Countries Around the World

Morocco

Nick Hunter

www.raintreepublishers.co.uk
Visit our website to find out more information about Raintree books.

To order:
☎ Phone 0845 6044371
🖷 Fax +44 (0) 1865 312263
🖳 Email myorders@raintreepublishers.co.uk

Customers from outside the UK please telephone +44 1865 312262

Raintree is an imprint of Capstone Global Library Limited, a company incorporated in England and Wales having its registered office at 7 Pilgrim Street, London, EC4V 6LB – Registered company number: 6695582

Edited by Abby Colich and Megan Cotugno
Designed by Philippa Jenkins
Original illustrations © Capstone Global Library Ltd.
Illustrated by Oxford Designers & Illustrators
Picture research by Liz Alexander
Originated by Capstone Global Library Ltd.
Printed in China by CTPS

ISBN 978 1 406 23565 4
16 15 14 13 12
10 9 8 7 6 5 4 3 2 1

British Library Cataloguing in Publication Data
Hunter, Nick-
Morocco. -- (Countries around the world)
964'.053-dc22
A full catalogue record for this book is available from the British Library.

Acknowledgements
We would like to thank the following for permission to reproduce photographs: Alamy: pp. 5 (© nobleIMAGES), 18 (© Christine Osborne Pictures); Dreamstime.com: pp. 30 (© Mypix), 32 (© Abdul Sami Haqqani); Getty Images: pp. 7 (Slow Images), 9 (Nat Farbman/Time Life Pictures), 10 (Abdelhak Senna/AFP), 22 (John Chiasson / Liaison Agency), 23 (AIDA/AFP), 24 (Abdelhak Senna/AFP), 29 (Bob Thomas); iStockphoto: pp. 19 (© rest), 21 (© Witold Ryka), 28 (© John Woodworth); Jacques Descloitres, MODIS Land Rapid Response Team, NASA/GSFC: p. 15; Photolibrary: pp. 25 (Françoise Lemarchand), 35 (Nicolas THIBAUT), 39 (Dallas and John Heaton); Shutterstock: pp. 6 (© Seleznev Oleg), 12 (© Dainis Derics), 17 (© Alexey Bykov), 20 (© hagit berkovich), 26 (© Freeshot), 27 (© Martin Maun), 31 (© Elzbieta Sekowska), 38 (© Africa Studio), 46 (© Kurt De Bruyn).

Cover photograph of a tree and a man in a green robe, Essaouira, Morocco, reproduced with permission from Photolibrary (Tim Durham).

We would like to thank Shiera S. el-Malik for her invaluable help in the preparation of this book.

Every effort has been made to contact copyright holders of material reproduced in this book. Any omissions will be rectified in subsequent printings if notice is given to the publisher.

Contents

Some words are printed in bold, **like this**. You can find out what they mean by looking in the glossary.

Introducing Morocco

Morocco is a country where many different **cultures** meet. Morocco is located in North Africa where the Mediterranean Sea meets the Atlantic Ocean. The northern tip of the country is just a few miles across the **Straits of Gibraltar** from the southern tip of Spain and the continent of Europe.

The North African country's location has shaped its unique history and culture. Morocco's population of more than 30 million people has been made up by different groups who settled there over the centuries. **Berbers** settled in the area thousands of years ago. Later, Arabs arrived from the east. More recently, people from France and Spain and settlers from south of the Sahara Desert have influenced Morocco.

All have created a rich and varied culture in Morocco – from the crowded streets of Morocco's ancient cities to its traditional food and music. And much of it is rooted in the religion of **Islam**, which was brought to Morocco in the 600s by eastern Arab settlers.

Challenges to face

Morocco also has many issues to face. Large numbers of its people still live in **poverty** and many cannot read and write. **Climate** change and lack of water are damaging Morocco's farms. In 2011 people in many countries in North Africa, including Tunisia and Egypt, demanded changes to the way they were governed. Morocco was also affected by the mood of change in the region.

YOUNG PEOPLE

Morocco is a changing society. Young people in the cities are influenced by traditional culture and religion, but also by what happens in Europe. Western clothes are replacing traditional Moroccan dress, and many young people travel to France and Spain to work.

Tradition is still important to many Moroccans, but people are also impatient for change.

History:
an independent nation

Morocco's history is a story of resistance to control by other countries. The first **Berbers** probably settled in Morocco about 8000 BC. The Sahara Desert then had more **vegetation**, and the early Berber people raised animals such as cattle.

Early history

The Mediterranean Sea was home to great civilizations. The **Phoenician** traders came from present-day Lebanon and set up ports on the coast of Morocco. The Phoenician city of Carthage, in modern Tunisia, controlled the area. In 146 BC Carthage fell to the armies of ancient Rome. Rome ruled Morocco for many centuries.

The arrival of Islam

From 681 AD, eastern Arabs came to Morocco. They brought a new religion called **Islam**. This religion would shape Moroccan life forever. Moussa ibn Nosair conquered Morocco in 705 and then conquered much of Spain and Portugal. Until 1492, **Muslims** controlled parts of Spain.

The remains of the Roman city at Volubilis still survive today. Volubilis was also the capital city of Idris I.

Many Moroccan cities have **medinas**, or ancient walled towns. Warriors from the Sahara founded the city of Marrakech in 1062 AD.

Idris I became the first king of Morocco in 789. Over the following centuries, Morocco was part of many Arab empires and kingdoms. In the 1400s, the **Ottoman Empire** conquered much of North Africa, but Morocco remained outside this empire. Portuguese armies were also driven out of Morocco at the Battle of the Three Kings in 1578. The battle was the end of European efforts to control Morocco for a while. In 1664 the Alawite **dynasty** of kings came to power. They still rule Morocco today.

For three centuries, Morocco was the only part of North Africa to stay outside the Ottoman Empire. The country gradually became isolated.

European influence

In the mid 1800s, France took over Morocco's neighbour, Algeria. Morocco battled to resist both France and Spain. In 1901 a new king Abd al-Aziz took power. He surrounded himself with European advisors and took on European ways. Moroccans were not happy. Unrest spread, and the Europeans saw their chance. France and Spain agreed to control Morocco. In 1912 most of Morocco became a French **protectorate**, with Spain controlling the north and south of the country.

The French built a new capital at Rabat, and Casablanca grew to become Morocco's main industrial city. Morocco was an important base for the **Allies** in World War II as they fought against German armies in North Africa.

The path to independence

When the war ended in 1945, many of the old European empires were coming to an end. Moroccans wanted to be independent. In 1956 French and Spanish forces left. Morocco became an independent country under King Muhammad V.

ABD EL-KRIM (1882-1963)

Abd el-Krim was the leader of a rebellion against foreign rule in Morocco. He organized tribes to fight a **guerrilla** war against Spain and France. In July 1921, el-Krim's forces defeated Spanish forces at Annoual. They formed the **Republic of the Rif**. The Europeans sent an army of 250,000 men to defeat him. On 27 May, 1926, Abd el-Krim surrendered. He was sent to live in exile and died in Cairo, Egypt, in 1963.

Casablanca was a small town before it was expanded by the French.

Morocco since independence

Since independence, kings from the Alawite dynasty have continued to rule Morocco. In addition to being a faithful Muslim, King Muhammad V thought that equal rights for women and a strong education system were important for the future.

In 1961 Muhammad died and his son became King Hassan II. King Hassan's long reign saw many changes in Morocco. Political reforms led to people having more power to elect the government. The reforms also kept the different parts of Morocco united.

Border disputes

In 1975 Hassan sent Moroccan troops to try and take control of Western Sahara, which had been governed by Spain. A long war followed between Moroccan troops and resistance fighters supported by Algeria. Although open conflict ended in 1988, the issue has still not been finally settled.

KING HASSAN II (1929-1999)

Hassan II was a skilled leader who managed to keep Morocco unified during a difficult period for many North African leaders. After becoming king in 1961, he introduced a **constitution** and reformed politics while keeping much power for himself. He was accused of treating opponents harshly and not respecting **human rights**. Overseas, he was friendly to Western countries and sought peace for Arabs and Israelis in the Middle East.

Morocco in the 21st century

Hassan II's son Mohammed VI, who became king in 1999, has faced many challenges, including **terrorist** attacks from **radical** Islamic fighters. They believe Morocco does not follow their strict form of Islam closely enough. In 2011 the king was forced to make reforms in the face of protests calling for changes in government.

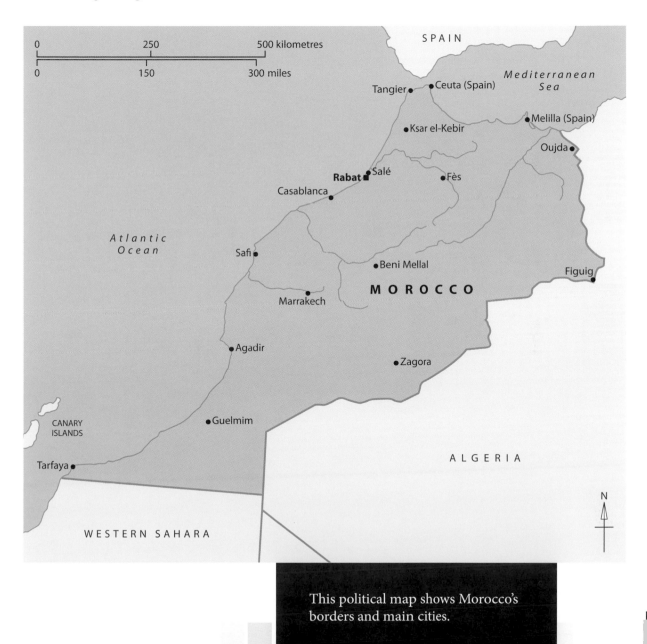

This political map shows Morocco's borders and main cities.

Regions and resources: land of contrasts

Morocco's land is more varied when compared to other North African countries. Its **terrain** ranges from forests and peaks of the High Atlas Mountains to the vast expanses of the Sahara Desert, which stretches across North Africa. The Sahara is the world's largest desert.

Morocco covers a land area of 446,431 square kilometres (172,368 square miles), with a long coastline on the Atlantic Ocean and Mediterranean Sea measuring 1,835 kilometres (1,140 miles). The country also shares a long land border with Algeria in the east and Western Sahara in the south. Spain is just a few kilometres away across the **Straits of Gibraltar**. Two Spanish territories, called Ceuta and Melilla, are on Morocco's north coast.

Morocco's coastal plain is **fertile**. Farmers get essential water from rivers that flow from the Rif Mountains in the north and the Atlas range further south.

The Atlas Mountains stretch across Morocco, Algeria, and Tunisia. Jebel Toubkal rises to 4,165 metres (13,674 feet) above sea level.

Earthquakes

Earthquakes sometimes happen on the edge of continents where different parts of Earth's surface, called plates, meet and rub together. Earthquakes cause the ground to shake and can destroy buildings. The Moroccan city of Agadir was destroyed by an earthquake in 1960. More than 12,000 people were killed. An earthquake near the city of Al Hoceima killed more than 500 people in 2004.

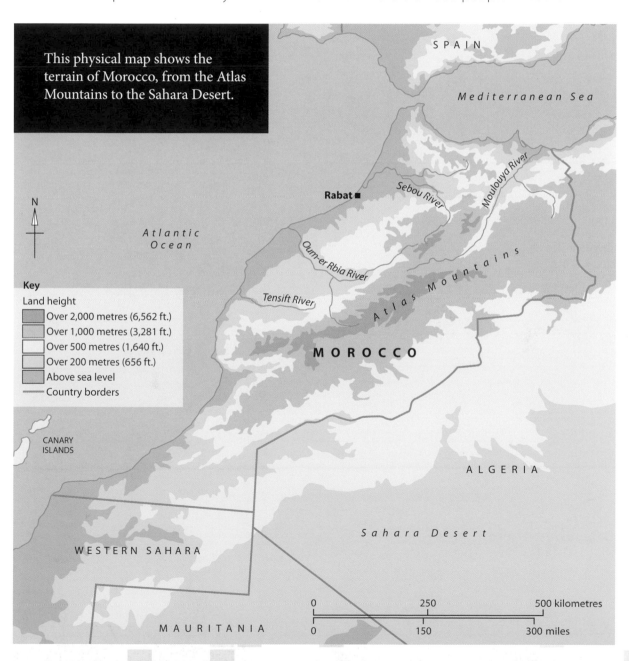

This physical map shows the terrain of Morocco, from the Atlas Mountains to the Sahara Desert.

SPAIN

Mediterranean Sea

Rabat ■

Sebou River

Moulouya River

Atlantic Ocean

Oum-er Rbia River

Tensift River

Atlas Mountains

MOROCCO

Key

Land height

- Over 2,000 metres (6,562 ft.)
- Over 1,000 metres (3,281 ft.)
- Over 500 metres (1,640 ft.)
- Over 200 metres (656 ft.)
- Above sea level
- —— Country borders

CANARY ISLANDS

ALGERIA

Sahara Desert

WESTERN SAHARA

| 0 | 250 | 500 kilometres |
| 0 | 150 | 300 miles |

MAURITANIA

Climate

The **climate** in Morocco is as varied as the landscape. Along the coastline, the climate is hot and dry in the summer, with milder temperatures in the winter. Most rain falls between October and April, and the total rainfall each year is greater in the north than it is in the south. Ocean currents can have an effect on the weather. The cold Canary Current in the Atlantic Ocean reduces the amount of rain that falls over Morocco.

Mountain climate

There is more rainfall in the mountains. The Rif Mountains in the north receive more than 2 metres (6.5 feet) of rain each year. Snow can cover the highest peaks for much of the year. This rainfall feeds Morocco's rivers, such as the Sebou, which flows 450 kilometres (280 miles) from the Atlas Mountains to the Atlantic Ocean. The 555-kilometre (345-mile) Oum er-Rbia is Morocco's longest river.

The climate is hotter and drier further south and away from the coast. Areas to the east of the mountains get almost no rain.

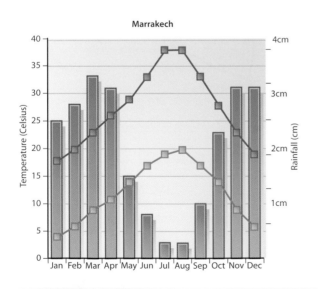

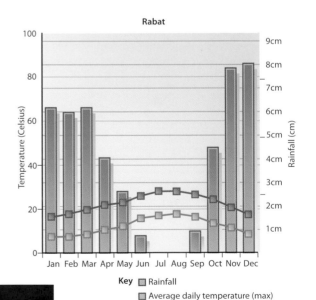

Key ■ Rainfall
■ Average daily temperature (max)
□ Average daily temperature (min)

These charts show the difference in rainfall and temperature between Marrakech and Rabat.

Climate change

Farming is very important in Morocco. Farmers rely on the rivers and enough rain to grow their crops. There is concern that more areas of Morocco are becoming desert and that this will continue as Earth's climate warms up. Most scientists believe that people cause this climate change. It will make it more difficult to grow food in Morocco.

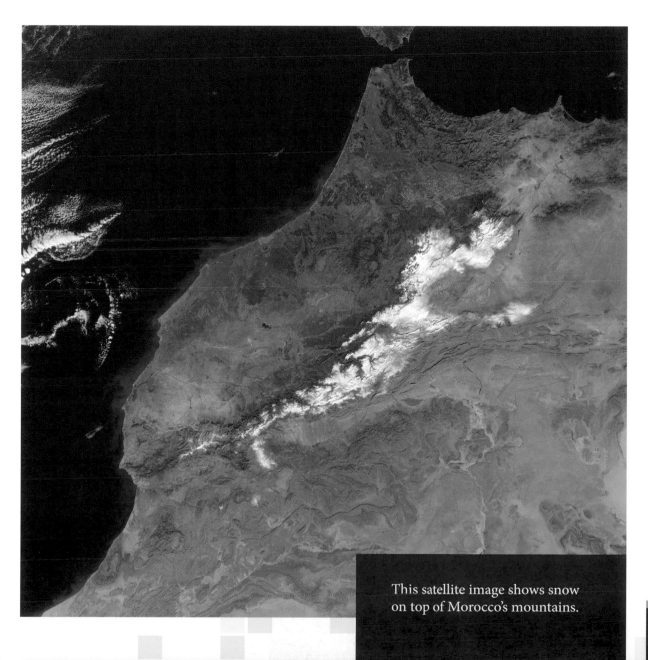

This satellite image shows snow on top of Morocco's mountains.

Economy and resources

Morocco's government is trying to modernize its **economy**. Many people live in **poverty**, and only around half of Moroccans can read and write. Industries such as clothing manufacturing and food processing are growing, but Morocco still has much work to do.

Morocco's main natural resources for **export** are phosphates. Phosphates are essential in making fertilizers used around the world to help crops grow. Unlike other North African countries, such as Algeria and Libya, large amounts of oil have not been found in Morocco.

Farming

More than four out of ten working people in Morocco are farmers. They grow crops such as wheat for local **consumers**. Fruit and vegetables are also exported to Europe. Morocco's location – just a few kilometres from Europe – and its warm southern climate allow for growing and exporting vegetables that only grow at certain times in colder countries. These are then sold in British and German supermarkets, for example.

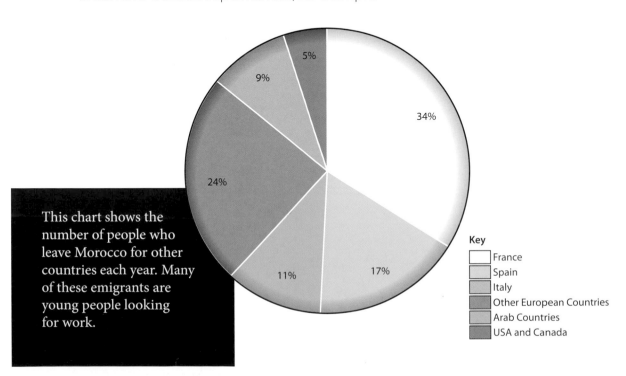

This chart shows the number of people who leave Morocco for other countries each year. Many of these emigrants are young people looking for work.

Key
- France
- Spain
- Italy
- Other European Countries
- Arab Countries
- USA and Canada

Tourism

Farming is not the only way that Morocco benefits from its short distance from Europe. Morocco is one of Africa's most popular tourist destinations. Tourists come not just for Morocco's warm climate but also for its history and **culture**.

Tourism is a growing part of Morocco's economy.

YOUNG PEOPLE

Finding a job can be difficult in Morocco's cities. Nearly one in three young people is unemployed. Many young people decide to move, or **emigrate**, to European countries such as France and Spain where they can find work.

Wildlife: between the ocean and the desert

Morocco's landscape varies from wild coasts to mountains and deserts. It is home to a huge range of wildlife.

The slopes of the mountains are lined with forests with many different types of trees, including Atlas cedar and cork oak trees. Many flowers, including irises, orchids, and geraniums, bloom in Morocco in April and May. They bloom just after the wetter winter and before the heat of summer. Shrubs, such as acacia, grow on the rocky and salty shorelines in the south of the country. Almost nothing grows in the dry desert because all plants need water.

Preserving forests

People are concerned that Morocco may be losing many of its forests. This **deforestation** is a result of cutting down trees for wood and clearing land for farming. Furthermore, forest fires are common in the dry Moroccan summers. Forests are important to bind soil together; without them, **fertile** topsoil can be blown or washed away by heavy rains. The Moroccan government plants many thousands of acres of forest every year to combat the threat of deforestation.

These trees in the Atlas Mountains are being cut down for their timber.

Plants and animals must endure difficult conditions to survive in the Sahara Desert.

Trees, such as the hardy Argan tree, are important in holding back the expanding Sahara Desert – this tree grows only in Morocco. If these trees die and desert conditions take hold, it becomes nearly impossible to grow anything. Desert **vegetation** is found only near **oases** in the south of the country, where date palm trees are common.

Animal life

In ancient times, lions and elephants roamed around in Morocco. Today there are a few panthers and jackals, but large **mammals** are far less common. Fennec foxes live in the Atlas Mountains. These mammals have adapted well to living in hot, dry **climates**. Thick fur keeps them warm at night and protects them from the sun during the day.

Found across North Africa and in Gibraltar on the southern tip of Europe, the Barbary macaque, a species of monkey, lives in Morocco's cedar forests. Morocco is also home to hundreds of species of birds, from eagles in the mountains to storks that enjoy the warm Moroccan climate in winter.

National parks

Morocco recognizes the importance of caring for its animals, plants, and landscapes. However, the twelve Moroccan national parks make up less than one per cent of the country's land. Threatened species in the national parks include birds such as the northern bald ibis. It can be seen in the Souss-Massa National Park in the south of Morocco.

Fennec foxes' big ears help their bodies to lose heat.

How to say...

Most people in Morocco speak Arabic and use a different alphabet from the one used in English. The following Arabic words are written as they would appear in the English alphabet:

desert	*sahra* (sa-ha-rah)	**mountain**	*jabal* (ja-bul)
sheep	*kharuuf* (ka-roof)	**tree**	*shajara* (sha-ja-rah)
monkey	*qird* (kerd)	**eagle**	*nasr* (nas-ur)

Birds, such as these white storks, are often seen in Moroccan cities in winter. In summer they live in the cooler climates of Northern Europe. They **migrate** south in the winter.

Infrastructure: the road to a modern state

Morocco is the only state in North Africa to be ruled by a **monarch**. King Muhammad VI is part of a family that has ruled Morocco for hundreds of years. The king still decides, with the advice of other leaders, who will be **prime minister** and who will lead different government departments.

Morocco has two houses of **parliament**. Morocco's people vote for members of the Chamber of Representatives every five years. Groups that include local councils choose members of the Chamber of Counsellors. Morocco's current system of government was introduced in the 1990s – a huge step in the modernization of Morocco.

KING MUHAMMAD VI (B. 1963)

Muhammad VI came to power in 1999 at the age of 35, following the death of his father, Hassan II. Muhammad VI introduced many changes in Morocco. He has allowed people and the media greater freedom to criticize the government. He has also tried to tackle **poverty** and has passed laws to give women equal rights. In 2002 King Muhammad married Salma Bennani, a computer engineer. The couple have two children.

These Moroccans are campaigning for democracy and **human rights**.

Islamic extremism

Islam is central in Moroccan society. Almost 99 per cent of Moroccans say they are **Muslim**. However, there are concerns that an extreme form of Islam is becoming popular. People who follow the religion's extreme form criticize the Moroccan government's friendship with the United States and the **European Union**, for example. Following the 2003 bomb attacks that killed several people in Casablanca, extreme Islamic **political parties** have been banned.

Morocco is still a relatively poor country. Many people, particularly outside big cities, do not have things that most **developed** countries take for granted, such as clean drinking water or healthcare. The Moroccan government has committed itself to reducing the gap between rich and poor.

Education and literacy

Elementary and secondary education is provided from the ages of seven to sixteen. Many young people, however, do not go to secondary school. Girls are often less well educated than boys. Despite laws promoting equal rights, many families do not expect women to work outside the home.

Only around half the Moroccan population can read and write. When compared to other countries in the region, Morocco is far behind.

Moroccan students are taught in Arabic. French is also taught as a second language.

These young Moroccan girls will most likely have to work to support their families, rather than go to school.

Literacy rates

The table on the right shows the percentage of people in North African countries who can read and write. The **literacy rate** in the UK is about 99 per cent – with little difference between males and females.

Country	Literacy rate (male)	Literacy rate (female)
Algeria	80%	60%
Egypt	83%	59%
Libya	92%	72%
Morocco	66%	40%
Tunisia	83%	65%

YOUNG PEOPLE

Often young people in Morocco do not go to school because they have to work. Girls living outside the cities are particularly likely to miss out on education. Poor families need the money children can earn working in factories and fields. Schools have to convince families that learning to read and write will benefit them.

Culture: where the Islamic world, Africa, and Europe meet

Morocco has one of the world's most exciting **cultures**. Without its location on the edges of Africa, Europe, and the Islamic world, this would probably not be true.

The people of Morocco

Morocco's people are mainly a mix of **Berbers** and descendants of the Arabs who brought **Islam** across North Africa. Berbers settled in North Africa thousands of years ago. They have a stronger influence on Moroccan culture than they do in other North African countries. Many people from Africa south of the Sahara also live in Moroccan cities. Some settle in Morocco, while others use it as a route to richer countries in Europe.

Many Berber languages are spoken in local communities, but Arabic is the main language of Morocco. French is also widely spoken.

Muslims go to the mosque for midday prayers every Friday. This mosque in Fes has welcomed worshipers for more than 1,000 years.

Daily life

Almost everyone in Morocco is **Muslim**, and the king is the country's religious leader. The royal family is believed to be descended from the Prophet Muhammad, the founder of Islam. While Moroccans are devout, the branch of Islam that most follow is less strict than the one practised in some other Muslim countries.

Away from Morocco's bustling cities, many people live in mountain or desert communities that have changed little for generations.

City life

Morocco is known for its bustling and exciting cities. Many old walled cities, or **medinas**, have been preserved in modernized cities such as Marrakech and Fes. Most of Morocco's large industrial cities – Tangier, Casablanca, and the capital Rabat, for example – are along the Atlantic coast.

Family life

Family is very important to most Moroccans and is often the centre of their social life. Traditionally families are large, but this is changing as young people marry later in life and more young women are finding jobs. Outside the cities, family groups are usually larger and more traditional.

In Islamic societies, traditionally women have not had the same rights or roles as men. Morocco has made great strides to make sure women have equal rights, but there are still some who feel these new rights are in conflict with the teachings of Islam. Nevertheless, in Moroccan cities, women often wear Western clothing and do many of the same jobs as men.

Daily life

Traditional Moroccan clothes are often beautifully woven and embroidered in many different colours and patterns. They include the *kaftan*, an ankle-length collarless dress with wide sleeves, and the *jellaba*, a hooded woollen cloak often worn by Berber tribesmen in the mountains. Today many Moroccans, particularly in cities, wear Western-style clothes.

Moroccan design and decoration is very distinctive, using bright colours and repeated patterns.

Sports

Moroccans often meet at the local café. There they might watch Morocco's national sporting obsession – football. Tennis is also popular. Moroccan athletes have had success at the Olympic Games.

GREAT MOROCCAN ATHLETES

- Nawal El Moutawakel (pictured) was the first woman from an Islamic country to win an Olympic gold medal when she won the 400 metres hurdles in 1984.
- Hicham el-Guerrouj won the 1500 metres and 5000 metres track events at the 2004 Olympic Games.
- Marouane Chamakh, forward for Arsenal Football Club and one of many Moroccans to play in top European leagues, is also the Moroccan team captain.

Daily life

Fresh fruit and vegetables, herbs, and spices are bought daily from the market, or *souqs*, in larger towns. In country areas, the market may be held only weekly. Prices are not marked, and Moroccans are used to bargaining with the seller.

Famous food

Morocco is understandably famous for its food. Meat and vegetables are cooked with different spices to create delicious dishes.

Moroccans usually eat their main meal at lunchtime. Meals may start with salads or soups, such as *harira*. This thick soup is often eaten in the evening during **Ramadan**. Ramadan is the Muslim month of fasting when people eat nothing between sunrise and sunset.

Couscous is a popular meal. This cracked wheat, a bit like rice, is served with meat and vegetables. In the south – or in poorer areas – couscous might be flavoured with onions and raisins instead of meat.

Moroccans also like sweets such as "gazelle's horns" pastries, which are desserts filled with almonds and honey.

Chicken tagine

Chicken tagine is enjoyed by many Moroccans. Ask an adult to help you with this recipe.

Ingredients
- 4 pieces of chicken, off the bone
- tomatoes, potatoes, carrots, or another vegetable, chopped
- spices such as coriander, parsley, black pepper, ginger, tumeric, and saffron
- ½ preserved lemon
- 1 small onion
- 1 clove of garlic
- 8–10 olives
- olive oil

Method

1. Soak the chicken in a mixture of lemon, garlic, spices, and oil.
2. Add the chopped onion and your other vegetables and cook over medium heat.
3. Add water to the sauce and leave to cook slowly on a low heat. A traditional **tagine** pot is used to stop the water from boiling away.
4. Add olives for flavour.

Festivals

Food is a big part of the many Moroccan festivals. Religious festivals include *Eid ul Fitr*, which marks the end of Ramadan. Each year, there are more than 600 *moussems*, or **pilgrimage** festivals, linked to local **saints**. Weddings involve the whole community and can last for days.

Moroccan music

Moroccan music, a crossroads of different styles, has influenced many western musicians, such as the rock group Led Zeppelin.

Moroccan classical music has been developing for around 1,000 years. It combines influences from southern Spain with Arabian stringed instruments and percussion. *Gnaoua* music is unique to the region. It was developed by freed slaves, brought to Morocco from countries like Mali and Ghana. Similar to American blues music, it is centred in the city of Marrakech.

Groups of traditional musicians often perform at weddings and other social occasions.

Moroccan musicians use traditional instruments, including flutes *(nay)* and longneck stringed instruments *('ud and gimbri)*. Drums are important and are sometimes made from terracotta pottery.

Dance

Each region of Morocco has different traditional music and dance. In the High Atlas Mountains, villagers perform the *abouach* dance around a fire. The *tissint*, or dagger dance, from the south is part of wedding ceremonies in the Sahara.

Literature and film

Internationally acclaimed writers, such as Paul Bowles, settled in the city of Tangier in the 1900s and connected with Moroccan writers such as Mohamed Choukri. Many local writers publish in French as well as in Arabic. Both young writers and young film directors have thrived thanks to a growing freedom of speech. Many new films and books expose the harsh realities of life in modern Morocco – and the exciting culture.

Morocco today

Morocco's rich **culture** is just one reason why the North African country has a bright future. Morocco's welcoming people, varied landscape, and warm **climate** have made it a popular destination with tourists.

King Muhammad VI has tried to tackle many of the country's problems. He passed laws to give more rights to women. He tried to improve education for all Moroccans. **Poverty** and environmental problems are more difficult to combat. Conflict also continues in Western Sahara.

Morocco and the world

Morocco has good relations with many countries. Some even say it may one day join the **European Union**. However, support for the West has not always been popular. For example, when the United States and the UK invaded Iraq in 2003, there was much criticism.

Morocco certainly has close ties with other **Muslim** countries. Since 2003 those who use violence to support their extreme beliefs have been a problem for Morocco. In addition to the Casablanca bombing, people from Morocco were involved in deadly attacks on train stations in the Spanish city of Madrid in 2004.

In 2011, following revolutions in nearby countries like Tunisia and Egypt, Morocco's leaders faced even louder calls to modernize and solve many of Morocco's problems. Moroccans and the world wait to see if Muhammad VI and his government can survive and satisfy these demands for change.

How to say...

Hello	*marhaban* (marr-hab-an)
Goodbye	*ila al'likaa* (il-al-likaac)
Yes	*na'am* (nahm)
No	*la'a* (le-ah)
How are you?	*kaifa haluka?* (kay-fa ha-look)
My name is...	*ana ismee...* (an-a is-mee)

Morocco adapts to modern life against a background of tradition and strong Islamic faith.

Fact file

Country name: Al Mamlakah al Maghribiyah (Kingdom of Morocco)

Capital: Rabat (population: 1,705,000)

Language: Arabic; also Berber languages and French

Religion: Islam (99%), Christianity or Judaism (1%)

Government: Constitutional monarchy with Chamber of Representatives (325 members) elected by popular vote, Chamber of Counsellors (270 members) elected by local councils and trade unions, king, and prime minister

Independence date: July 30 (Throne Day – date when current king came to the throne)

National anthem: "Hymne Cherifien" ("Moroccan Anthem")

Fountain of freedom
Source of Light
Where sovereignty and safety meet,
Safety and Sovereignty
May you ever combine!
You have lived among nations
With title sublime,
Filling each heart
Sung by each tongue
Your champion has risen and answered your call.
In my mouth and in my blood
Your Breezes have stirred both light and fire,
Up! My brethren, strive for the highest.
We call to the world that we are here ready.
We salute as our emblem God, Homeland, and King.

(Source: Reed, W.L. and M.J. Bristow, National Anthems of the World, Cassell, London, 9th ed, 1997.)

This chart shows the population of North African countries.

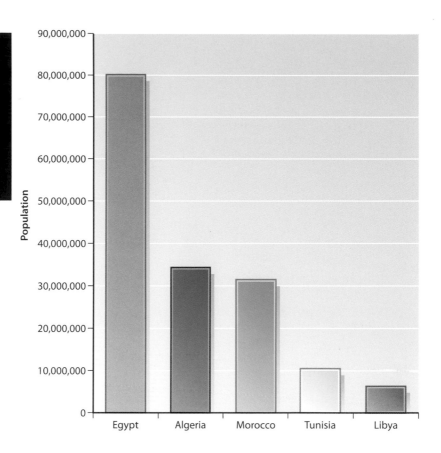

Population:	31,627,428 (est. 2010)
Life expectancy:	75.9 years (72.8 for men, 79.1 for women)
Bordering countries:	Algeria, Western Sahara, Spain (Spanish territories of Ceuta and Melilla)
Total land area:	446,431 square kilometres (172,368 square miles)
Largest cities:	Rabat, Agadir, Casablanca, Fes, Marrakech, Meknes, Tangier
Coastline:	1,835 kilometres (1,140 miles)
Highest elevation:	Jebel Toubkal, 4,165 metres (13,665 feet), in High Atlas Mountains

Major rivers:	Oum er-Rbia, 555 kilometres (345 miles); Sebou, 450 kilometres (280 miles)
Natural resources:	phosphates, iron ore, manganese
Imports:	oil and oil products, textile fabric for making clothes, telecommunications equipment, wheat, gas, plastics
Exports:	clothing and textiles, electrical parts, chemicals, fertilizers (including phosphates), citrus fruits, vegetables, fish
People below poverty line:	15%
People with Internet access:	33%; (Algeria: 12%; Libya: 5%)
Roads:	92,738 kilometres (57,625 miles) 57,396 kilometres (35,664 miles) paved
Famous Moroccans:	Muhammad Choukri (1935–2003), writer Abbas El Fassi (b. 1940), prime minister Hicham El Guerrouj (b. 1974), Olympic athlete Princess Lalla Salma (b. 1978), anti-HIV/AIDS and women's rights campaigner Nawal El Moutawakel (b. 1962), Olympic athlete, politician, and member of the International Olympic Committee

Almost half of Morocco's working people are involved in agriculture, growing crops such as these dates for food and to export.

Currency: Moroccan Dirham; 1 = 100 centimes

UNESCO World Heritage sites:

Medina of Fez: founded in the 800s and home to the world's oldest university

Medina of Marrakech: medieval walled city

Ksar of Ait-Ben-Haddou: typical Saharan town in southern Morocco

Historic City of Meknes: Spanish-style city built in the 1600s

Archaeological Site of Volubilis: ruins of Roman city

Medina of Tétouan: medieval walled city that was important as a link between Morocco and Spain

Medina of Essaouira: 1700s fortified town

Portuguese City of Mazagan: 1500s Portuguese settlement

A *ksar* is a traditional Saharan fortified town. Alt-Ben Haddou is on the eastern slopes of the High Atlas Mountains. The houses are grouped together behind high walls to protect them.

Timeline

BC is short for "before Christ". BC is added after a date and means that the date occurred before the birth of Jesus Christ, for example, 450 BC.

AD is short for Anno Domini, which is Latin for "in the year of our Lord". AD is added before a date and means that the date occurred after the birth of Jesus Christ, for example, AD 720.

BC

c. 8000	First Berber settlers living in Morocco.
c. 1000	Phoenician traders set up trading posts along Morocco's Mediterranean coast.
146	Phoenician city of Carthage falls to Rome; Morocco falls under control of Roman Empire.

AD

681	Arab invaders first arrive in Morocco and bring Islam.
789	Idris I becomes first king of Morocco.
1062	Marrakech founded by warriors from the Sahara.
1492	Muslims forced out of Spain; many settle in Morocco.
1578	Battle of the Three Kings forces Portuguese invaders to leave Morocco.
1664	Alawite dynasty of kings comes to power (still the royal family of Morocco).
1901	King Abd al-Aziz takes power and upsets Moroccans with his pro-European ways.
1912	France and Spain take control of Morocco; most of country controlled by France.
1921	Abd el-Krim's forces defeat the Spanish at Annoual and declare the Republic of the Rif.

1942	Allied troops use Morocco as base for campaign against German troops in North Africa.
1956	Morocco gains independence from France (March 2) and Spain (April 7); Muhammad V becomes king.
1961	Hassan II becomes king of Morocco upon death of Muhammad V.
1963	Moroccans vote in the country's first general election; parliament is suspended after two years due to political unrest.
1975	Moroccan troops occupy Western Sahara; a long conflict follows; region is still disputed.
1996	Revised constitution introduces two houses of parliament.
1999	Muhammad VI becomes king of Morocco on death of Hassan II.
2003	Many people die as a result of terrorist bombings in Casablanca.
2004	New family laws give more rights to women.
2009	Abdelkader Belliraj, said to be leader of terrorist group attacking Morocco and countries abroad, sentenced to life in prison.
2011	As protests sweep across North Africa, thousands of Moroccans protest in favour of greater democracy and reform of the legal system. On 21 February, King Muhammad VI announces a new Social and Economic Council to carry out reforms.

Glossary

Allies forces that fought against Germany, Italy, and Japan during World War II, including Britain, the United States, and France

Berber people, also called Imazighen, who lived in North Africa before the arrival, in the 600s, of Arab settlers from the east

climate usual weather conditions of an area

constitution written document describing how a country is governed and who governs it

consumers people who buy goods and services

culture customs and beliefs that are shared by a group of people, such as language, food, and music

deforestation removal of trees from an area, which can have a major impact on the environment

developed country where industry and the economy are advanced, often including wealthier countries such as the UK and the United States

dynasty family line of rulers of a country

economy how a society creates, uses, and distributes goods

emigrate leave a home country in order to stay permanently in another country

European Union association of countries in Europe that work together for free trade and agree on many issues

export ship goods out of a country for sale in another country

fertile suitable for growing things, for example ground that contains water and nutrients

guerrilla any armed group that is not part of a regular army, usually fighting against a larger force or invading army

human rights rights that every person has, regardless of who they are or where they live

Islam religious faith of Muslims, based on the text of the Koran and teachings of the Prophet Muhammad

literacy rate percentage of people over the age of 15 who can read and write

mammal class of animals in which the young are fed with milk from their mothers

medina traditional Arab town enclosed behind walls

migrate move regularly from one region to another, usually by season

monarch king, queen, or emperor

Muslim follower of Islam, or having to do with a follower of Islam

oasis (pl. oases) area of refuge in the desert

Ottoman Empire large empire based in the city of Constantinople (now Istanbul in Turkey) that ruled much of the Middle East and North Africa from the 1200s to the 1900s

parliament group of people that makes and approves the laws of a country. In a democracy, the people elect the members of parliament.

Phoenician relating to ancient people from present-day Lebanon and southern Syria, who traded along the coasts of the Mediterranean Sea

pilgrimage journey to a respected or religious place

political parties organizations that want to influence the government

poverty condition of being poor

prime minister government leader

protectorate country under the protection and rule of another country

radical extreme or wanting extreme change

Ramadan month of fasting, from sunrise to sunset, during the Muslim year

Republic of the Rif government in Morocco led by Abd el-Krim from 1920 to 1926

saint person thought to be holy and thought to be in heaven after death

Straits of Gibraltar narrow channel of water that connects the Atlantic Ocean to the Mediterranean Sea

tagine Moroccan dish named after the clay pot in which it is cooked

terrain type of land in a region, for example, rocky terrain

terrorist anyone who seeks to achieve political goals through violence

vegetation plants and trees

Find out more

Books

Africa (World of Music), Andrew Solway (Raintree, 2008)

Foods of Morocco (Taste of Culture), Barbara Sheen (Greenhaven Press, 2011)

North Africa and the Middle East (Modern World Cultures), Jeffrey and Charles Gritzner (Chelsea House, 2006)

The Middle East and North Africa (Regions of the World), Neil Morris (Heinemann Library, 2008)

Websites

news.bbc.co.uk/1/hi/world/middle_east/country_profiles/2431365.stm
This timeline of Morocco's history on the BBC website has been updated with recent news about the country, and has links to BBC news stories.

www.bbc.co.uk/learningzone/clips/playing-the-darbukkah/6786.html
The Moroccan musician Ghninou gives a demonstration of how to play the darbukkah.

www.historyforkids.org/learn/islam/religion/
This site has information on the history of Islam and other sections, including African history.

Places to visit

The best way to find out about any country is to visit the country and meet its people. That's not possible for most people. But if you are lucky enough to visit Morocco, check out the UNESCO World Heritage sites listed on page 39.

One way you can find out about Moroccan culture is to visit a Moroccan restaurant to get a taste of Moroccan food. If there is not one near you, you could borrow a recipe book from your library and try some North African recipes yourself.

Further research

There are many topics that can be linked to a study of Morocco.
- The countries of North Africa share much of their history and culture. Find out more about Tunisia, Algeria, Libya, and Egypt to discover the similarities and differences between Morocco and these countries.
- This book only has space to give a few details about Morocco's many styles of music. Try finding out more about some of the styles of music found in Morocco.
- Many young Moroccans travel to France and Spain to look for work. Try to find out more about their experiences of living overseas. Why did they leave home, and what challenges do they face?

Topic tools

You can use these topic tools for your school projects. Trace the map on to a sheet of paper, using the thick black outline to guide you.

The national flag of Morocco was adopted in 1915. It has a red background with an interwoven green star in the middle. Red symbolizes the royal family and green is the traditional colour of Islam.

N

■ Rabat

Index

Titles in the series

Afghanistan	978 1 406 22778 9	Japan	978 1 406 23548 7
Algeria	978 1 406 23561 6	Latvia	978 1 406 22795 6
Australia	978 1 406 23533 3	Liberia	978 1 406 23563 0
Brazil	978 1 406 22785 7	Libya	978 1 406 23564 7
Canada	978 1 406 23534 0	Lithuania	978 1 406 22796 3
Chile	978 1 406 22786 4	Mexico	978 1 406 22790 1
China	978 1 406 23547 0	Morocco	978 1 406 23565 4
Costa Rica	978 1 406 22787 1	New Zealand	978 1 406 23536 4
Cuba	978 1 406 22788 8	North Korea	978 1 406 23549 4
Czech Republic	978 1 406 22792 5	Pakistan	978 1 406 22782 6
Egypt	978 1 406 23562 3	Philippines	978 1 406 23550 0
England	978 1 406 22799 4	Poland	978 1 406 22797 0
Estonia	978 1 406 22793 2	Portugal	978 1 406 23578 4
France	978 1 406 22800 7	Russia	978 1 406 23579 1
Germany	978 1 406 22801 4	Scotland	978 1 406 22803 8
Greece	978 1 406 23575 3	South Africa	978 1 406 23537 1
Haiti	978 1 406 22789 5	South Korea	978 1 406 23551 7
Hungary	978 1 406 22794 9	Spain	978 1 406 23580 7
Iceland	978 1 406 23576 0	Tunisia	978 1 406 23566 1
India	978 1 406 22779 6	United States of America	978 1 406 23538 8
Iran	978 1 406 22780 2	Vietnam	978 1 406 23552 4
Iraq	978 1 406 22781 9	Wales	978 1 406 22804 5
Ireland	978 1 406 23577 7	Yemen	978 1 406 22783 3
Israel	978 1 406 23535 7		
Italy	978 1 406 22802 1		